To the memory of Dr. Mary Nell Saunders

Brief Mass

(SSAATTBB Chorus a cappella)

I. *Kyrie*
II. *Gloria*
III. *Credo*
IV. *Sanctus*
V. *Agnus Dei*

by

Dan Locklair

ISBN 0-7935-6976-1

e. c. kerby ltd.

DISTRIBUTED BY

HAL•LEONARD®
CORPORATION
7777 W. BLUEMOUND RD. P.O. BOX 13819 MILWAUKEE, WI 53213

Like the basic bread and wine elements of Mass, the fundamental musical materials of **Brief Mass** are simple. Yet, like the profound and eternal meanings of Mass, the use and development of the musical materials strive for deeper musical dimensions. The pitch material of each movement is basic, very limited, and does not stray from its foundation pitches. Each individual movement serves as a vital link to the whole of the work. Throughout its duration symbolism is invoked (including numerical symbolism), and the Holy Number 3 is the inspiration for each movement's three-part structure. While the ultimate aim of this work is the successful musical illumination of one of the most significant texts in the world, technical dimensions of each movement are now briefly described.

I. Kyrie
Joined by a common unity note, C, each of the soprano and alto voice parts (as well as the tenor and bass parts) share common exchanges of line. Metrical shifts occur through development of 4 3 5 3 meters. The sole pitch material used is a six-note synthetic mode: C, E, F-sharp, G, A-flat, A.

II. Gloria
This movement divides the choir into two separate SATB choirs. While not necessary for performance, it is suggested that the choirs be separated to enhance the antiphonal effect. In this joyous and highly rhythmical **Gloria**, a recitative-like quality permeates the entire movement. The sole pitch material used, forms a transposed Phrygian Mode: F-sharp, G, A, B, C-sharp, D, E, F-sharp.

III. Credo
As in movements **I** and **V**, meter development is employed here. Unlike **I** and **V** (which use the half-note as the unit of beat), here the eighth and quarter notes are the unit of beat as the meters alternate between triple, duple and triple time. Often using common, unison pitches to symbolize the united spirit of the Credo, this movement is centered around the new pitches B-flat and E-flat (thus, added with the pitches of movement's **I** and **II**, the total 12 pitches of the chromatic scale are now represented). The sole pitch material used in **III** represents a transposition of movements **I**'s pitch material: E-flat, G, A, B-flat, B, C.

IV. Sanctus
This double-chorus movement seeks to express a simple, hymn-like Sanctus, often of restrained joy. Like **II**, no metrical development is employed but, also like **II**, a seven-note mode is employed, this one being a synthetic mode made up of a combination of the Lydian and Phrygian Church Modes. The sole pitch material for **IV** is: A, B, C-sharp, D-sharp, E, F, G, A.

V. Agnus Dei
Like **I** and **III**, metrical development is an important part of this movement. The entire metrical structure of **V** is an exact retrograde of the meters of **I** with, again, the half-note representing the pulse. Musically, also like **I**, the **Agnus Dei** seeks to express pleas in a manner that is both restrained and ethereal. Like **I** and **III**, its primary pitch material consists of a transposition of the same six intervalic patterns: F, A, B, C, D-flat, D. In addition, the 16th century **Genevan Psalter** 12th Psalm (a Psalm of plea) tune, **Donne Secours**, is freely quoted in the men's voices. While based on the same pitches as the entire **Agnus Dei**, the Psalm tune also incorporates two additional pitches, E and G, which serve to further musically unite this movement with movements **I** and **III**.

PERFORMANCE NOTES
Brief Mass requires a minimum of eight singers for performance: SSAATTBB. It is suggested that the singers be divided into two separate SATB antiphonal choirs. This separation, while possible in concert performance, may not be possible or practical within the context of worship and this is left up the conductor's discretion. Whether or not the choirs are separated, the composer suggests the following set-up since it will serve all possibilities with ease.

I	II	
Tenor/Bass	Bass/Tenor	Soli Deo Gloria
Soprano/Alto	Alto/Soprano	D.L.

Timings:	I-ca.	3:00
	II-ca.	2:30
	III-ca.	3:30
	IV-ca.	3:00
	V-ca.	3:00

Total Duration: ca. 15:00 minutes

To the memory of Dr. Mary Nell Saunders

Brief Mass

Dan Locklair

I. Kyrie

Slowly with a floating, ethereal quality (♩ = ca. 52)

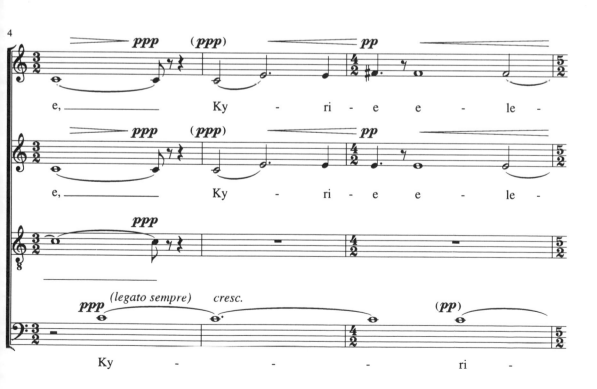

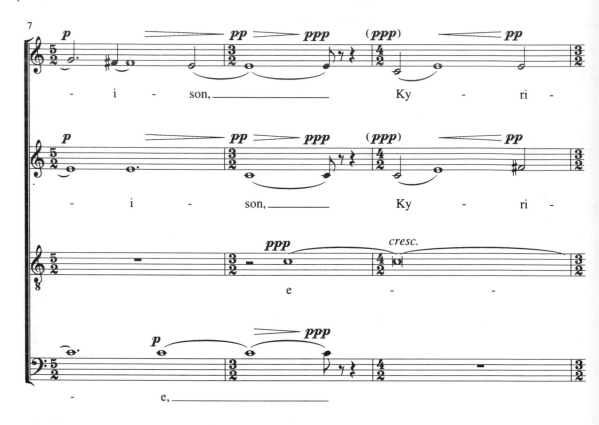

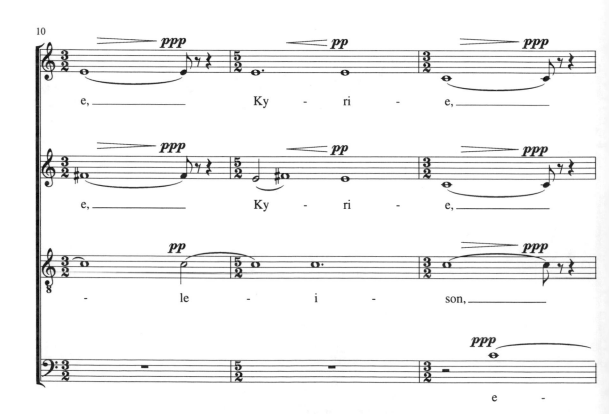

6

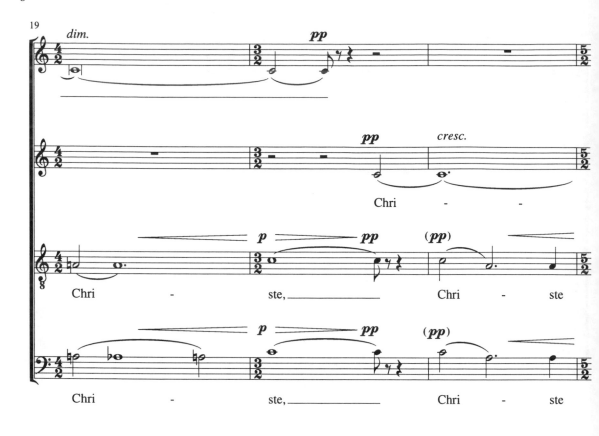

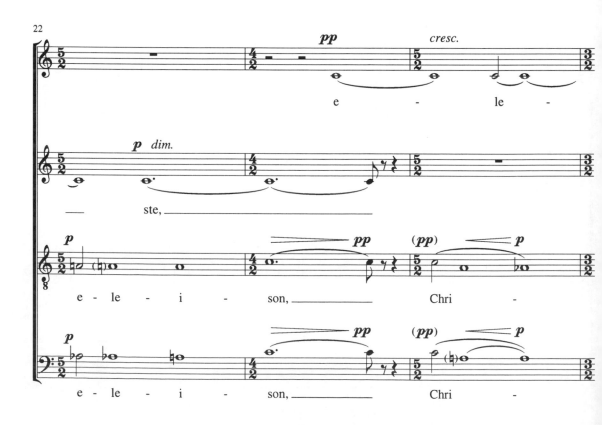

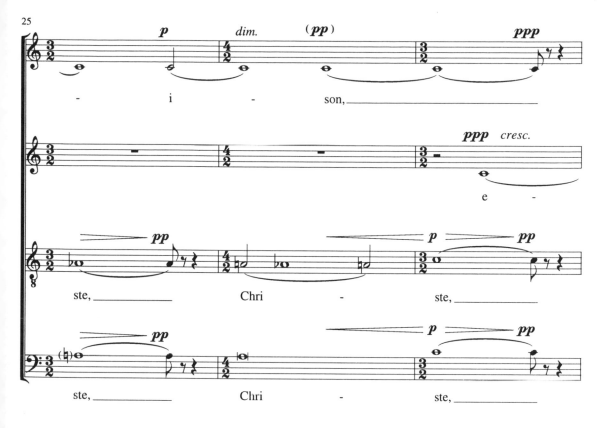

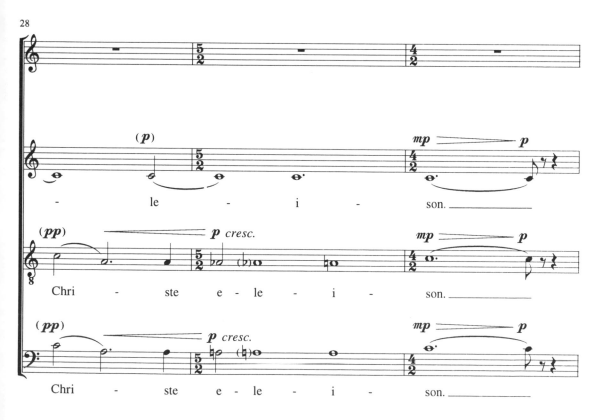

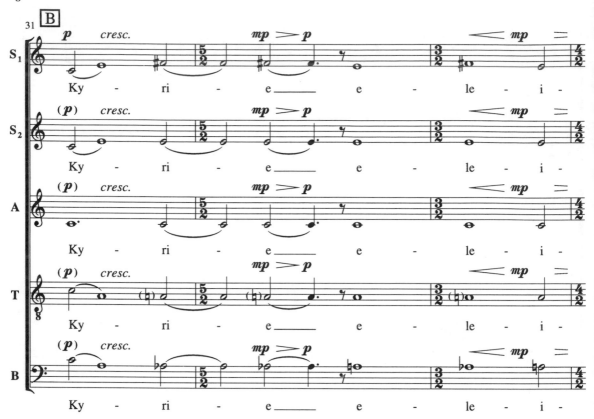

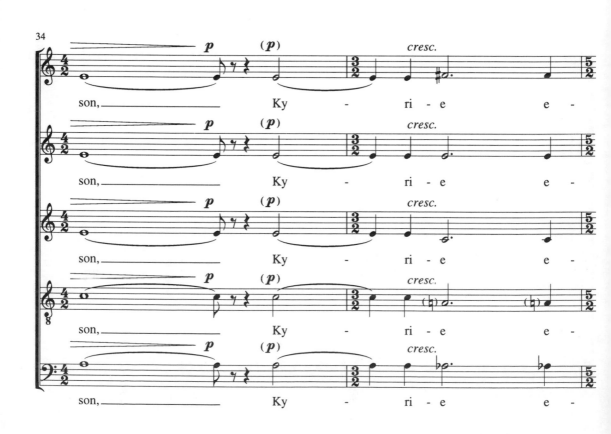

*Full section or solo. If sung by a soprano soloist, other Soprano I singers
  should sing the Soprano II part beginning on the 4th beat of measure 36.

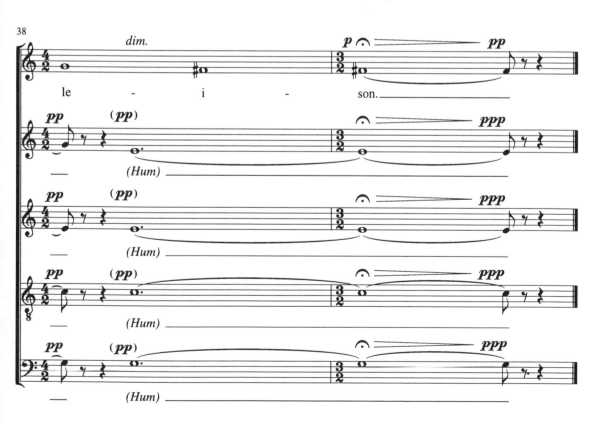

II. Gloria

14

- ne Fi - li u - ni - ge - ni - te, Je - su Chris - te, Je -

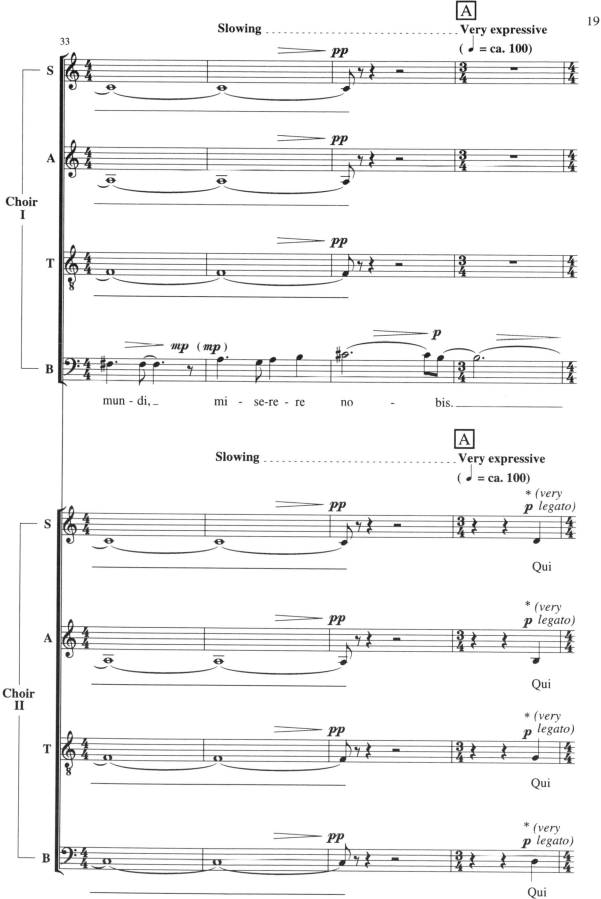

*If the conductor so chooses, solo quartets may sing until measure 69.

20

*If the conductor so chooses, solo quartets may sing until measure 69.

23

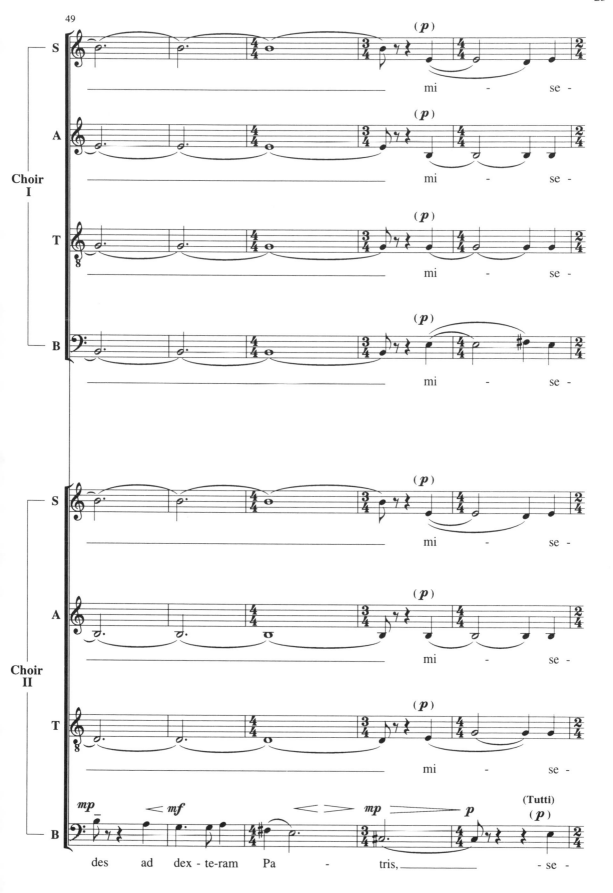

30

III. Credo

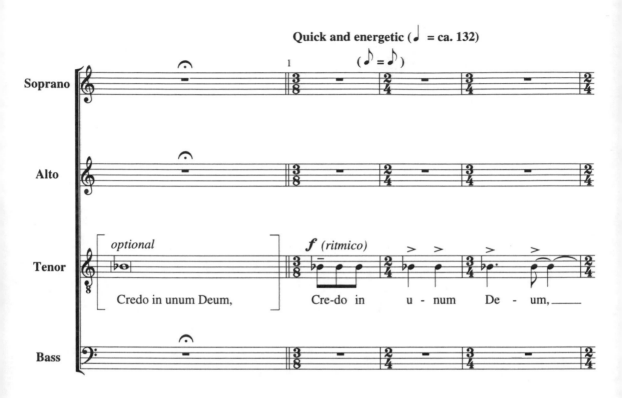

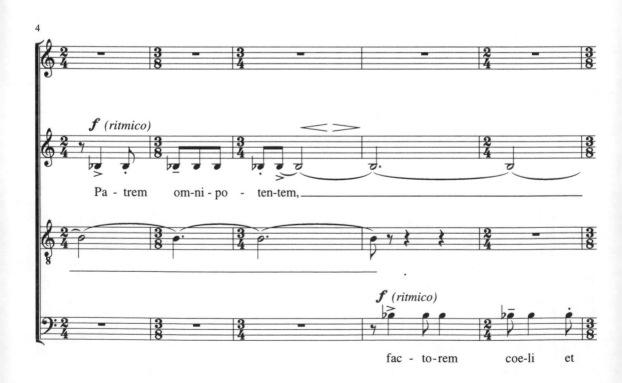

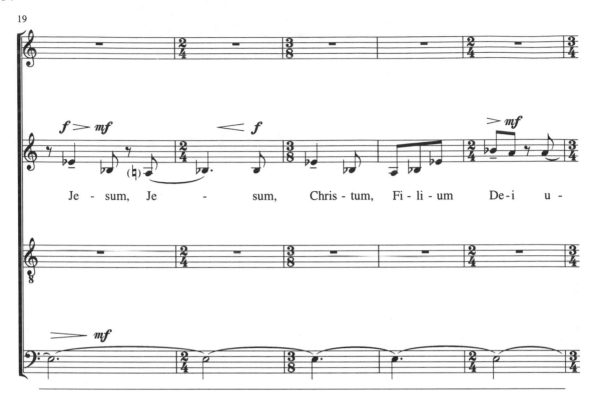

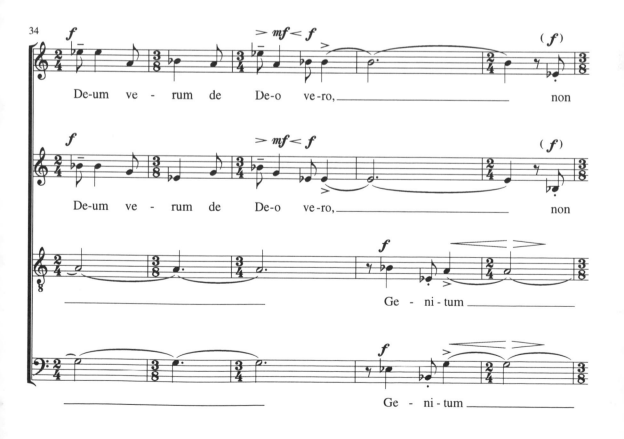

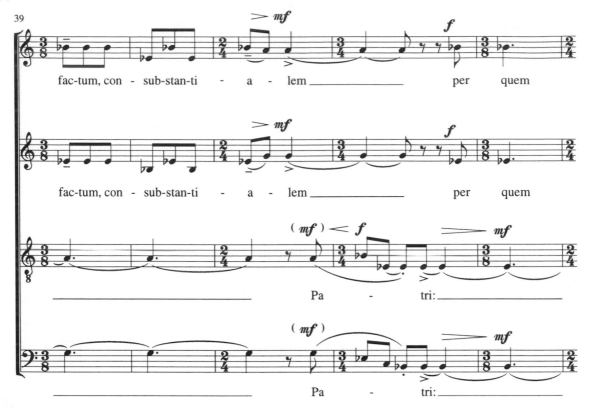

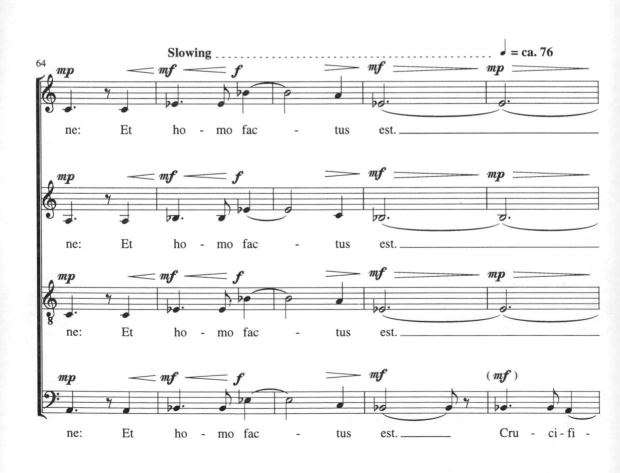

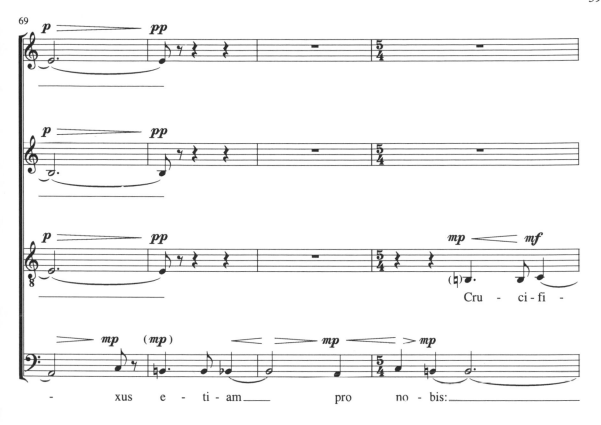

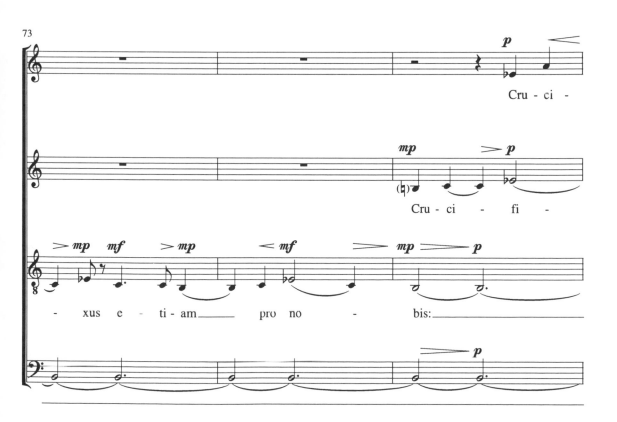

fi - xus e - ti - am pro no - bis: sub Pon - ti - o Pi -

- xus e - ti - am pro no - bis: sub Pon - ti - o Pi -

e - ti - am pro no - bis: sub Pon - ti - o Pi -

e - ti - am pro no - bis: sub Pon - ti - o Pi -

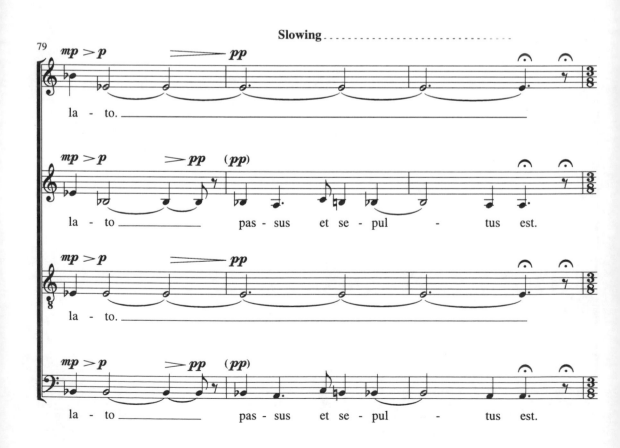

Slowing

la - to.

la - to pas - sus et se - pul - tus est.

la - to.

la - to pas - sus et se - pul - tus est.

B Quick and energetic (♩ = ca. 132)

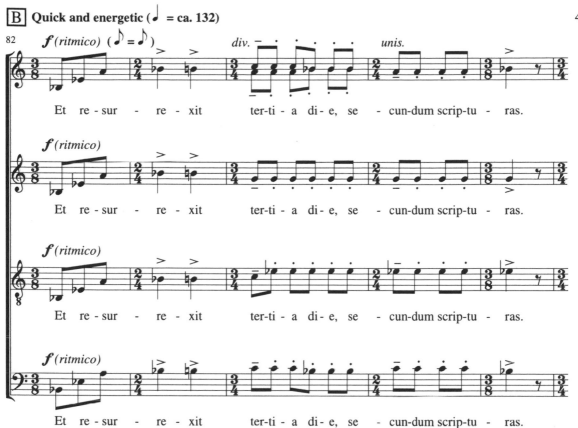

i - te - rum ven-tu-rus est cum glo-ri- a, glo-ri- a, ___ ju - di -

i - te - rum ven-tu-rus est cum glo-ri- a, glo-ri- a, ___

i - te - rum ven-tu-rus est cum glo-ri- a, glo-ri- a, ___ ju - di -

i - te - rum ven-tu-rus est cum glo-ri- a, glo-ri- a, ___

ca - re vi - vos et mor - tu - os ___ non e - rit

cu - jus re - gni non e - rit

ca - re vi - vos et mor - tu - os ___ non e - rit

cu - jus re - gni non e - rit

ma   in   re - mis - si - o - nem   pec - ca - to- rum.

Et   ex - spec - to   re - sur - rec - ti - o - nem   mor - tu - o - rum.

IV. Sanctus

*Choir II

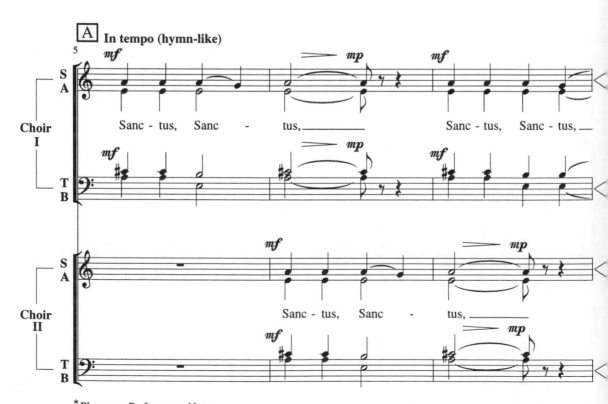

Choir I

Choir II

* Please see Performance Notes
  for divisi suggestions.

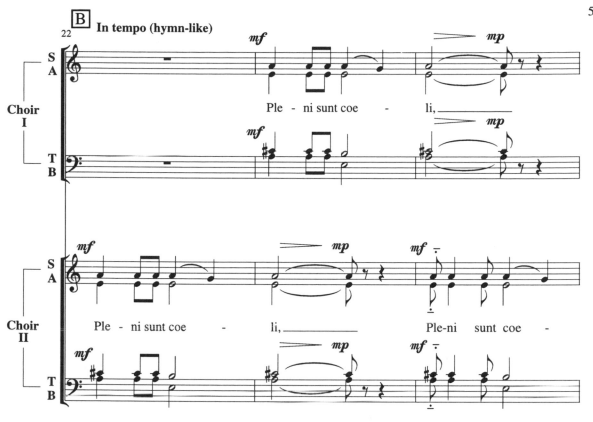

54

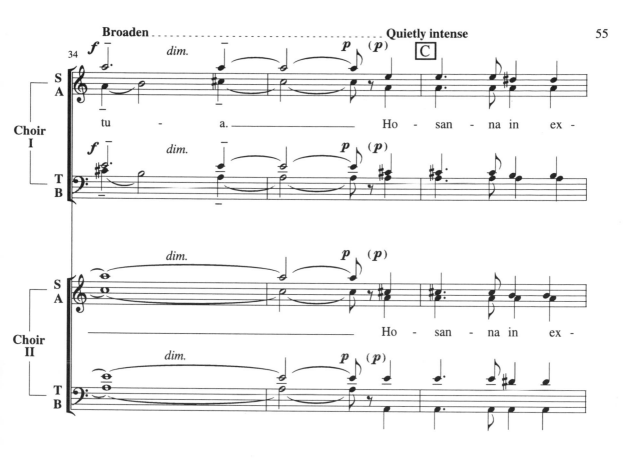

(Broaden)

D **Simply - like the beginning (hymn-like)**

58

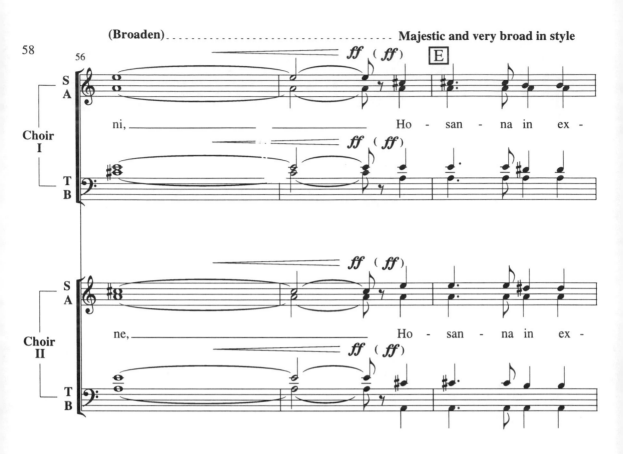

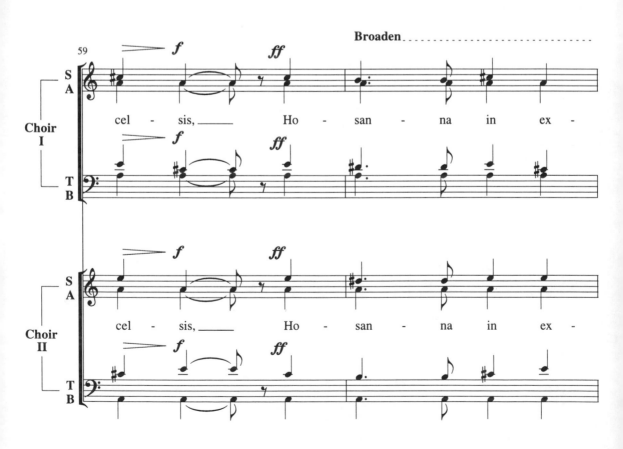

Slower tempo (𝅗𝅥 = ca. 42)

V. Agnus Dei

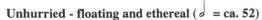

Unhurried - floating and ethereal ($\half$ = ca. 52)

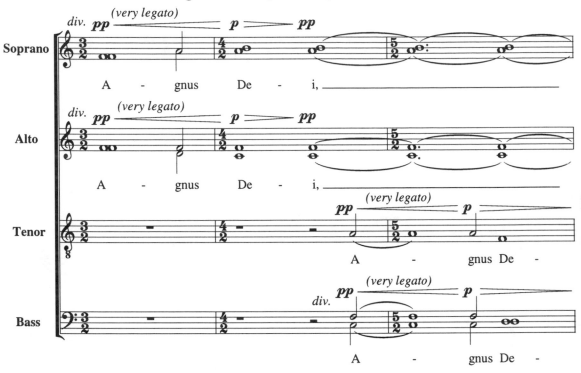

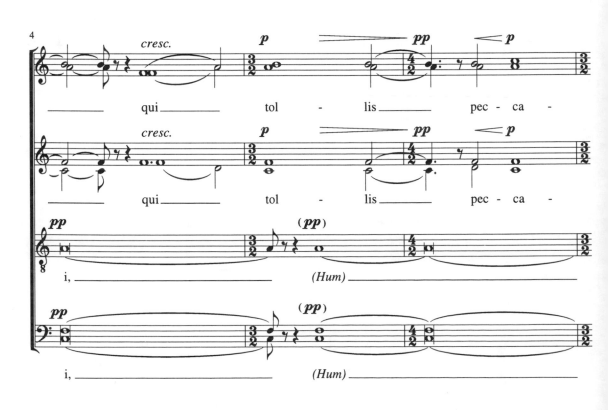

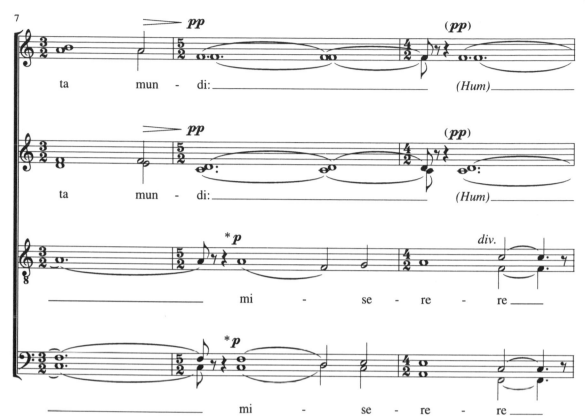

*The 16th century Psalm tune, DONNE SECOURS (GENEVA 12) is freely quoted in the tenor and bass parts. From Louis Bourgeois's GENEVAN PSALTER (1551), the tune is associated with a Psalm asking for the Lord's help: Psalm 12.

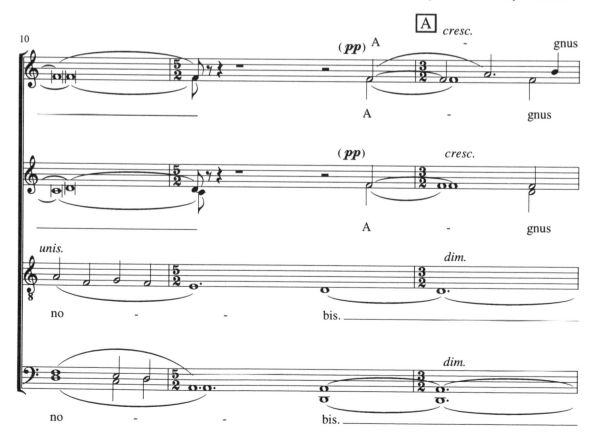

De - i, _____ qui tol - lis, qui tol -

De - i, _____ qui tol - lis, qui tol -

_____ (Hum) _____

_____ (Hum) _____

_ lis pec - ca - ta _____ mun - di: _____ (Hum) ____

_ lis pec - ca - ta _____ mun - di: _____ (Hum)

mi - se -

mi - se -

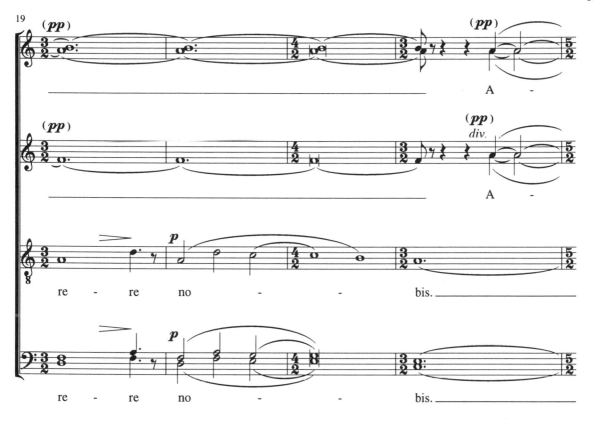

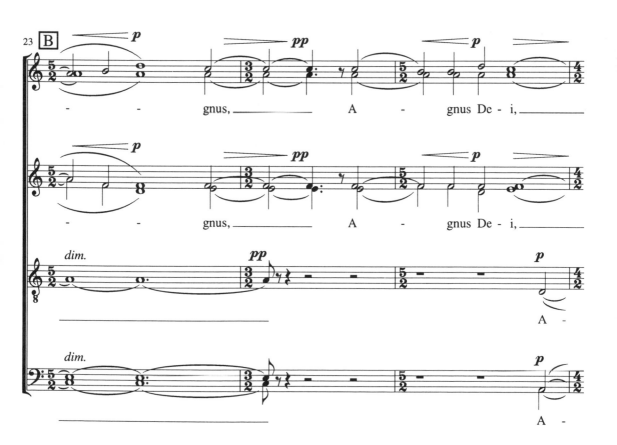

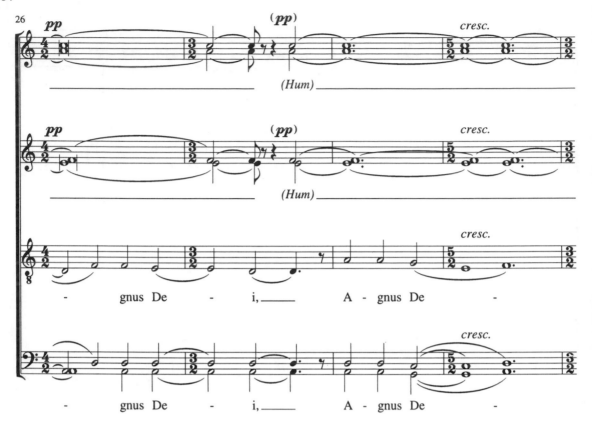

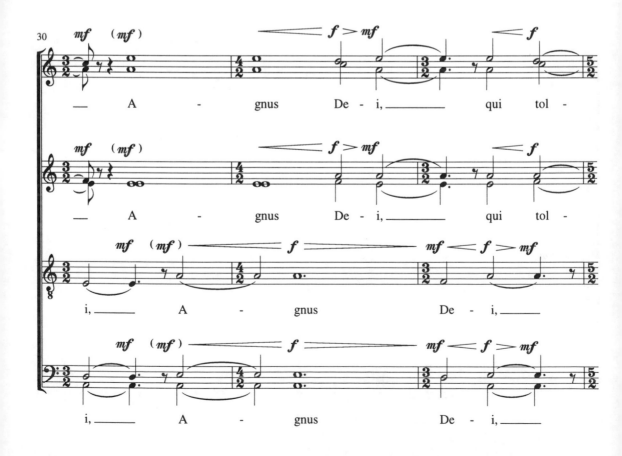

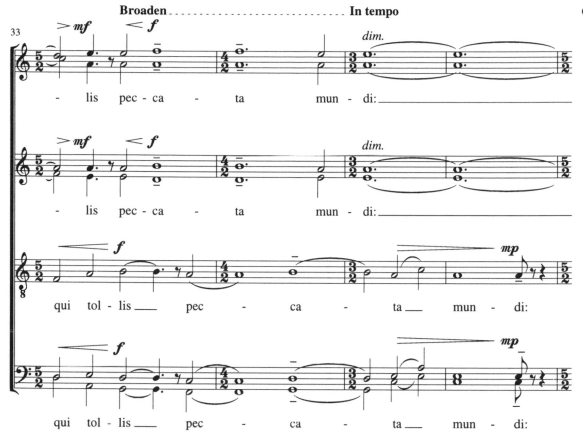

May 1993, Winston-Salem, NC